MILES PRESS

Indiana University South Bend Department of English

THE MIMIC SEA

South Bend
Oct. 2012

Charmi,
Please come to
Florida and protect
me from the zombies
and bath salts!

[signature]

42 Miles Press

Editor, David Dodd Lee

Copyright© 2012 Erica Bernheim. All rights reserved.

ISBN 978-0-9830747-2-4 (pbk. alk. paper)

For permission, required to reprint or broadcast more than several lines, write to:

42 Miles Press, Department of English, Indiana University South Bend

1700 Mishawaka Avenue, South Bend, IN 46615

http://42miles.wordpress.com

Art Direction: Paul Sizer, Design: Dimitri Theodoropoulos, Production: Paul Sizer

The Design Center, Frostic School Of Art, Western Michigan University.

Printing: McNaughton & Gunn, Inc.

THE
MIMIC
SEA

POEMS
BY
ERICA
BERNHEIM

For my parents, with love

CONTENTS

The fish, too,
*   Are afraid of the sun*
Under the half-stacked greens of the rotten bridge,
And light falls with the ultimate marigold horror:
*   Innocence.*
*   The fish fin-flutter able*
Unable to hide their secrets any longer: what they know of Heaven
*   As stars come down   come effortlessly down   down*
Through water.

—James Dickey, from "The Zodiac"

What lies before me is my past

—Oscar Wilde, from "De Profundis"

I

Moonrats

Anyone can tell you I'm bad news, can
see the reflections of those fireworks
in the shadows of different pavements.
True, words were never spoken.
The problem is I knew you back
when your hands were under a hundred
and even then it was hard to keep up.
How do you measure something
determined to pass over the world?
You walk like reincarnation,
each movement unbearably tedious,
inexplicable, predictable, staving off
your self with both hands. I would placate
you in a blessed sack for the rest
of your days, associate your self with
fire, with the yellow and red cross
of St. Andrew, and what they'll find,
digging up that street, bone-slow and heavy.
Explain to me disappearance, the
vanishing of fingernails after a long
bath, something I could pin my wishes
upon other than parfait's glycerin treats,
or octopus, old turf, turning white with
sleep, devouring my arms to protect
you. Anymore, my heart resembles the adhesive
of a child, easily passed off as something
else—somewhere, buried under the framework
of a phony construction site, the unbearably
twilight stench of other people's urine. All
I can thank you for is expediency, renting,
and paying the actors to watch over you

until morning, losing your last few teeth,
and reading on. Like, for instance,
sitting across from you with nothing to say.
I have forgotten how it means to be so tired.
It's good to notice, like naturalness
in ballroom dancing: a spin to
the right, men with names like
Nick Cotton and the women's heads, oh,
to see that angle while still alive, only
seeming broken. You need not be moving
to love this much speed, a chemical tang of lust.
It's about execution: waltz, tango, quick-
step, slow fox trot. Nick Cotton gets rid
of his tails. A pretend swoon at the end,
the woman is almost to the floor, my
grandmother cries out, "Kiss her!" I am
planting morning glories at night. I can
regenerate anything but this: nothing
from nothing, more nothing than nothing.
But these are high holy days without
you, something curling under the doorways
like smoke, no, don't call it that, call it dolore,
like God, when he cared enough to be
vengeful, and watched the effort of closing
your lids over the globes of your downturned
eyes, the vision so crisp and mistaken, days
of keratin and roses will make you see.
Elements. Hello, neighbor. I think nothing
of leaning into your photoed face, sad darling,
I've got rights and I should look into them.

Chicago Day Lily

Left alone and watered less, it flowers
into the nightmare tarnished dreams I
predicted would come for me next. Tender
me your loose change. Afford me purchase
of your maps. To grasp the centermost
spectacular of the lily is to think of the possible,

that this city misses you already, the expressway
of alleged serpentine delight awaits your tendered return.
This season allows itself the luxuries of clothing
askewed, seeing through these dirty tricks
we will do again and then once more. Prehensile
and filthy, the slickness of the nervous bulb

permits it to dream cyclically of the light above.
This genre of clemency is well deserved, and
without it, we'd not breathe, humble Kansan
refusers of such a story. The absences are real,
decoys for precious exits through soil that bleeds
hues of toothpaste and swimming pools, real colors

with missing eyes. Sunshine is the new currency,
the reminder we foretold would bring predictable
gestures, the nuance of the sound, the grasping
at whatever's easiest, in front of you, take it, best
and worst decisions—like sadnesses we let linger—
too long across decay's hesitant deep plane.

Darwin Light

When a train goes too fast,
it shakes. You must slow your
self, like you know what two
o'clock means. A stewardess
and her Xanax will easily be
parted, even sugar and cream
is a less natural combination,
even the sight of an old woman
putting on lipstick makes me cry,
my eyelashes black stucco, your
hands become rays again, flat and lethal.
I could place you in the middle of
those tracks, set you down, tiny, and
walk away. I was invisible and now
I am just fading. I was among
people I could not speak to and pressed
my fingers through a bruise
because there was nothing
to get stuck on. I saw those
behind me die with eyes no one
knew about, I lost sight of you, the moon
abandoned the sun, agreed to leave
the moon alone and not call so late.
I am feathered, alone. What I want:
twin squid babies suckling my tomorrows
the way deeply sour candy still tastes good
—to have that clamp around the heart—
two squids, four eyes, one with smaller feet.
Love depends on its moment of arrival,
the moment they began to split. Or maybe
too late, a lady with piss-colored hair

is struck from the curb and hits her face against
the gutter in December, puts her hand
to your belly and tells you luck has nothing
to do with the You In There and one day
these twin boys will be tall men who run
around tracks, spaces that seem wide open,
shifting like bad narrators. Who follows me
with swansdown, gray boxes with 3-D borders,
silver-tongued fountain pens, a magnifying
glass so scratched it would reverse itself
to work again. Nothing here is all right, no
one wants to go home. When I lived
on land, not even the sea would forgive me.
Tell me about other abodes, trailers wide
enough for two of what, the ice in a snapshot,
different kinds of holes—over-warm and smelling
of motor oil. Show me where you built
this hutch, how someone else filled it
with plastic forks and a Sears catalogue.
Hold still. I will know your wishes,
if you can move time. I am tied
to this monster. And you think
of worlds and cut-glass families,
transparent and clean, sharp like motion.
There is nothing abstract in that laughter.
There is nothing for us to talk about.
I want nothing from you, save tongue.
You are nothing to me, save muse.
My knees are pressed together like
an Egyptian girl with wafers on her lips. I am
beginning to dislike the man with the whip.

If you hear of me, I might say no listening
allowed. Just like that, on faith, on hope,
on chastity. I fail miserably. Whatever you put on
first is full of air, digital bibles, cunning
methods of listing the sins of your fingers.
Blow up this beautiful emptiness and set
the tableau in Mexico: we should have sold
out. An unknown reason named you
is the cause of this, and I trip on the stairs
but nothing falls out of place. Eclipse
means abandonment.

Bunny Ohio

I wanted nothing more than to clothe you,
to wrap your wounds in fear's rope, put you
by that window, its view of so many Japanese
beetles, shiny foil coats glinting like plasticine
olives. Imagine me as the magician's rabbit:

being nothing, introduced as emptiness,
hiding under felt-warm layers,
my arrival the best sort of surprise,
an expected one, and my
departure is their optimism;
this crowd can believe

I waited in another dimension
and was summoned from a garden
with very thin air. Imagine what I touched
was only an outside, then a bumper crop
of faces and hands pushing at nothing,
my surprise is they create sound at the sight
of me, then marvel at my summoned absence.

It is only fair to be accurate;
I tell you I have done this trick
many times. I mean it.
It is only to tell you: I am still a resident
of this state: something terribly
wrong will find you. Don't worry
about the continent holding your heart,

and help me, help me, never to be like you.

The Mimic Sea

after P.T. Barnum's name for the early aquarium

The insomniac is immediately identified, thanks to the prickly
taste of her eyelids. Cats dream the same dreams as all other cats.
Nemesis plants flourish beneath glass, best remembered for their
vindictive natures, always re-staking and dividing the nobility of their
own last claims.

I already know how you are, he says before having placed
so much as a foot to the gear. And I know what has happened.
What we have in common is that we used to be our best
selves in other people. We wore clothing made by people
who cared nothing for us.

You can't have too much blood. From the outside, this sea forces
us to imagine it, and this allows the FeeJee Mermaid to stay with
her keepers, Silence and Chastity. See this monkey's torso, sewn
to the body of a fish, useful as typewriter ribbons, as strumming
a guitar with claws better suited for butter sauce. Cramming our
own bones down our own throats, sucking out the marrows with the
abject intimacy we learn to mimic.

When you hear the explosion from above, you will know it
was me. When our mouths flash open beneath each other's, it is
to scrape clean these barnacles of imaginary travel, signs that we
might be always alone and happiest that way. Beckon to us, fabulons
and tire swings, noisemakers and mufflers, a list of places I've stood

outside unhappily: a weather-stripped barn, two glass walls crammed with bubbles, a tired sea unaffected by my need to leave it in pieces, a fragment answering to Desire, a note left behind is to be called nothing.

The ambrotypes are, if you try, tongue-traceable, their wishes masked under layers of glass compassionate only to itself, protecting the finny miscreants trapped on both sides. Protection and its baggage will soon be parted. These are names to be recalled: perch, starfish, anemones, periwinkles, sunfish, carp, sea ravens, flounders, rays, jellyfish, pickerel, sticklebacks, horned pout.

Looking at them, you know they will not survive long. Imagine how many whales—albinoed, mistaken for porpoises—gave of their own best selves to stay with them in waters aerated but never changed. Buoyancy is its own best punishment.

An excuse for need, for knowledge, prior, unwanted and demonstrated daily, thanks to the addition of a hand organ and the seal who thinks he can play it well. It is true I have struggled.

Think how long you can make the same mistake without trying. Notice how slowly water moves when it explodes around something so huge. Wait for it to stop.

Like a Face

Any tale of spontaneous human combustion
must take place in the south. History's wagon carries
me in its horrible mouth of an entryway. An arrow
relies on less, taste this, rising from the swollen
finger raised to measure air's currents.
The girl allergic to water battles for acquagenics.
Sweat, blood, saliva and tears blister her skin.
She bends her head for the most dangerous of kisses.
She drinks whole milk and is allergic to her
own body. She will dream of swimming and touching
snow. Her lips feel as close and sharp as razors, the light
explodes, and you surrender your addiction to No-Doze.
Something in breath dies slowly, a fern, a stilted horseman,
a moon seen in daytime, or this harvest gone rotten badly.
How long will you stay in this mess, waiting to learn
when to duck, when it's safe to run: a plate of eyelashes,
a walk on water, nothing more. Loving days.
A maze with no entrance, and we strain to see
it anyhow. I find myself on the wrong side of your
affections, afflictions, you say, and suddenly these are
sidelines. I tell stories so often, I don't remember the event,
signs written in languages I never learned to read.
What I told you made no difference, lighthouse, philosopher,
my sleep. Oh, it trickles down the side of
a bed I never meant to lie in. Say something
about the state of dedication. What I wish for you
is nothing but fraud and petulance, camphor in
your proceedings, a brick in your mailbox, a wicked
bitter woman stealing your truck. I hope you can
believe this is not about you. You wake up
to find you've been tying your shoes with a dead man's
hand. You try to build a fire beneath a chimney
with no flue.

Anne Boleyn

"The people will have no difficulty in finding a nickname for me.
I shall be Queen Anne Lackhead."
—Anne Boleyn, upon learning of her impending execution

Who would have guessed
it was you and brother George
who invented the French Kiss
across someone else's deathbed.
Perhaps this is how we
grow up: six-fingered and
a birthmark on the neck can
mean a witch, but one who holds
out, doesn't give so easily,
until realizing three years later
no one is indispensable, not
even the head of a kingdom
who will be ruled by uneven bodies.
What is wrong with a voice
that wants only opera? Work.
Pleasure in work. You
were not fair. Skin changes color
to show emotion. Yours
remained sallow. Your final threat,
Anne, the seven-year drought,
did they know then? Each
number like a calculator's,
formed from the pieces that made
each previous now unnecessary.
If the word "picnic" had existed,

would you have chosen this life?
Another king died from peaches
and new cider; there were poisons
that asked for months to impregnate
clothing, letters, and cooks were meant
to sample everything or be themselves
boiled. The luxury of privacy.
The taste of your future. Every birth
becomes a death sentence. You may
bring food to an execution, but
you must pin up your hair so as not to
interfere with the blade. Death, quickly.

Nightdoctors

A grave must be robbed within ten days
of burial, a simple but back-breaking process.
Medical students in eighteenth-century
London had to supply their own cadavers.
Discovery was the enemy;
they were often beaten by the families
of the deceased. You can recognize
the words and not understand the sentence.
What is the only other option,
kneeling beside a grave, anabolic
minds reminding them why and how
we must learn to learn without bleeding,
without cutting into what we've taken
such pains to resurrect. Best to define this
as love not ringing true. A broken finger,
a horse's tail, the forgotten end of a hedgehog,
always open, always proof of your crimes.

Somewhere in Sussex, in his bedroom,
a small boy is lifted by these thoughts.
One day, people will scramble to fetch things
for him, and he will never sit near a bright window
again. He will think of darkness and the feel
of his fingernails against a burlap death sack,
how they catch against the rough edges,
the one whose legs swung to the ground
when he ran with her, and it seemed to him
the earth beneath her naked feet gave of her,
her bumping against him in quick time.

Car Rolls Off Clay Wade Bailey Bridge

And what of the driver, trapped between metal
and more metal, metal and water, water and time?
A concrete island, a wish for loosening,
a confrontation with his mother nineteen
years ago, too close to tell anybody, now
bored by tears in this condition of you,

abandoned, outside of town, it comes to us
quickly, northbound. Think of it as a loop
bound to a tunnel, cautioning an electric cathedral,
weakness, a hipbone resting against what you call
a tree seen near water. Imagine yourself named.
Listen to yourself shutting both up and down.

Imagine yourself, remembering daylight savings
for once, only better, your only knowledge is
one of desire and now it can be just. You
forget to breathe, and this, look, moving, this
does it for you. Icicle lights. Fountain gates.
Pressurized air locks more than enough you

into you. A shrapneled soldier who wants only
to go back is worth that trouble. Think of the gun,
oblique and finite, rushing in as though water
could change to pears and honey. If it's me
you're here for, say so, Cincinnati, listen,
if you were beautiful, there'd be no need for this.

The One Who Shot Me

was reading aloud before it happened:
"I dreamt I was a controversy."
Like a pool party to watch the world
burn, we were evacuated on a Tuesday,
saved on Friday by oysters, snappers,

groupers, but no blowfly; she stays behind.
The antidote was worse than knowing
I wanted this. Violence, you six-shot-
deal. I remember the oven you

purchased. Name one:
I forget trying to remember
to clean it. Hat, you have become
a hand. Bullet, I thought you
knew me better than that. Hand,
I mistook you for a stop sign.

The One Who Shot Me Next

didn't wear sunglasses. He looked good
in whatever he wore, but he wasn't wearing
yellow. He wasn't at the park. He wasn't
at the mall. I heard he was at the movies.
It was true. He was watching the scene

when access to parking spaces becomes
less likely than thinking about it.
Baroque, coded, straining, and vengeful,
your best-kept secrets, murmur beneath
a bridge under a wall. Patrons dream
of daydreams of bedbugs and haze, yet

we will never agree on how it happened.

Pavese Said Death Will Come Bearing Your Eyes

It is late at night
and you are making
soup for other people.
There are wool sweaters
in piles around your
ankles and your nose
seems full of blood.
A little boy brought
a newspaper for you
today; it was bright
and cold. You were
thick and unlovely until
your body hit the
water. Now. When cops
lie, you call it the
blue wall. You will
develop a great true
love for the metronomes,
placing them on the
shelves of your closets,
keeping track of your
frequently silent comings.
Automatic, quiet, more
of everything. When the
season begins, these
girls you know will all
buy Bibles, creatures of
habit. You are not
ready for a reunion,
whatever it is. Who-
ever made this room

knew his flashes of
brilliance wouldn't last
much longer, so he
painted in huge colors
and couldn't bring himself
to buy a watch. Your
father's dead, and it
is late. Even
dishonest people become
involved in terribly
disappointing ventures,
and you say this is one,
this is for your grace.

63rd and Pulaski

It has been you I have wanted to look at,
proving my faithfulness to my home away
from home: the appendix: something I can
live without. I had forgotten there were stars

this bright, forgotten that blocks can be
arranged and counted, their absence a reward
for sleep, their presence a reward for seizing.
The coast is gone; the ocean comes back

to us, it mouths its phosphorescence the way
destiny licks an ankle, then moves away. In
this city, seagulls greet me in the oddest places:
a supermarket parking lot, an underpass

passing for a tunnel, next to scaly pigeons
who circle finely with no shrapnel in their legs.
The seagulls whip and strain around them
by train tracks. We fall against nothing. We turn

to stone. We smolder in sunlight. Out
of respect for the gloves, the glass stays clean.
How lucky we are that others who go don't
want to come back. At noon, the grocery store

closes its doors, the sun begins to tarnish,
nights with you are not nights at all, says
one seagull to the pigeon. No, she replies,
your head goes best in the way of leaves.

The Responsibility for Everything That Breaks

The bargains we make in our heads, we say, are for sea
changes, never anything capable of enduring our wishes.
Plasticine rests against the willing tongue like the cost of

handbags, prescient and showy, handles loosened and slack.
They know the shape of your words, what you will need and
when your hands will enter them. From what is left, I yearn

for that, your taste of glue. You are seated among benches.
Booths may be there, but no one needs them. No one asks
the bodies what will become of these farms of them, how

long it might all take to mend. Some days after we leave
you for dead, another begins speaking again. They all talk
to each other. They realize what will happen, that the words

are what flutter their hands back around our suspiciously
inclined necks: incomplete, excrementious, disaffections.
I know many of these things are meant to be completed:

the visualized calculation of each probability, have met:
what it means to run off the path of a motorcade presidential
in nature, the mouth, accent like a hatpin poised above

thousands of punks sledding down staircases that can end only
in treachery. When I hear truth chances nothing, I learn
I am composed of barnacles and height. I move in shattered

chains linked by the powerless and broken transmitters.
I solder you apart, shattered guardian of toilet seats and endless
sealants for our wounds opened like clam mouths, traps that trap

nothing: two pairs of spectacles, the lounging barrier, don't blink,
but these must be the two ugliest horses at Saratoga. And they
breathe and they remain, themselves past all desire hybrid

in its blooming, dreams remembering their offspring. How
was it stamps became so important? Happy, this day of the
dead horses, the myth whispered, the well-greased moral:

that what you want will learn to want you back, that the best
skies promise little to voices that dream of being recalled.
Hints fall like linens from handbags, ornaments from shelves,

legs jammed through heat vents. How much happier we are
with our clothes on! How delightfully we antique from one
blossom shellacked, to what we leave behind in pieces pleads

no contest. Fixing you will not bring me to or away from
myself. You must learn to love what I do to survive. You
will want what I have fixed. I learn to hate what desires me,

what and how and why desire does me, hushes me, lest this
ether trowel be a lens too scarce and knowing. No cure can
exist without a miracle. Chords anymore count for so little.

You should say this, looking at me surreptitious and quarantined,
thinking of Throwdown Central, please please never come back here.

Dinner—June

This is excitement.
These are your dreams.
Given space, a catfish
grows to fit it. This
is about your father and
his curious love for chorus
girls and aspic. His friend's
name is Arthur, and he is a
Viennese pastry chef. This is
Ron, lips pressed to a Jeep.
This is Ben, carrying a
shoebox. You would have
disappeared until his father
came back, bringing spaghetti
and bacon, and it's suddenly three
in the morning and it's still
raining and you're on the porch,
attached to space like catfish expanding
and decaying, wrecking scales
against the limits of this bad love.
This might be when you asked why
batters close their eyes when they
swing, and anymore, I'm too uneasy
to disagree tonight. Bruised, you
continue, and his father says take these,
they're like Valium and you have no argument,
nothing more to say. Back inside,
you are a wooden chair in a cold house
with little other furniture and you are
naming in the dark, falling off that chair
and Arthur is bringing you more food

to fall for, little things cut into cubes,
and you think, this must be the first
time I have tasted this, only to mean
throwing garbage at America, beginning
with Los Angeles and star-spangling
your way to Tennessee, calling
from what sounded like heaven
to ask about those who won't
open their eyes, who won't look
at what's headed their way. What
is another name for soft deceit.

Virgil Moon

I'm willing to bet that greasy twenty
stuck to the bottom of your empty
file cabinet, it's never me you think of
when you try to shoot yourself
onto the ceilings of your apartment.
Your thoughts lie somewhere in the sink
you call your Amazon Basin, soapy home
to blue Julies and banded Lisas and frozen
Charlottes, their spiny tongues making short
work of crumpled toothpaste tubes
and tiny spoons and the questionable
ghost of your mother's lover who kicked
your dog across state lines, showing little
more remorse than a teenage shoplifter.
Last night I dreamt you took out the
trash, flipped beautiful lean burgers
on an outdoor grill; I can see you talking
to the plumber, convincing him to lose
himself down the slimmest of pipes
in search of what we've discarded
and still cannot move past. Without
you, I dream of blood in my stomach,
my breath shrinking when jewelry
salesmen beckon enormous topazes
in my direction, and I am always tempted
to move towards that city which has yet
to discover neon. It is my turn to bask
in the limelight. My turn, Tabasco.
The lime's light, and this glass so heavy.
Pretending we have been pensive, all bets
are often decided by the sea star, stomach

flowing out its mouth, straight to
the point, that food, nothing gets wasted,
save a few starfish, one backed against the
wall, tube feet straining to make sense of
a truck that refuses to shift into reverse, and
is still going nowhere fast, a bad phrase,
a neck in the creek, a tiny piece of skin,
determined not to let you love it, or ever
be able to give it up. Watch out
for this, super-mouth, skullcap of bald, you
don't have to adjust your ill-fitting pants to know
everyone's looking down, and there's everything
you could do about it and won't. The gum I pull
from well-tractioned heels clings like a
cinnamon-scented animal, who knows what it
doesn't know yet is worse than being
stepped on. I'm sorry for still thinking of
you, for wanting to clip your nails with
left-handed scissors for no reason other
than to be difficult, to repeat an old
man's mantra in your ugly ears while
you pretend not to be asleep, "The bench
is in the church, the bench is in the church."
Virgil Moon is willing to see my bet
and raise us both, straighten our legs,
and get our minds out of the soap
dish, but the line at his window is too long.
Tell me something dreamy and hopeful,
why Virgil Moon's hair is in such
disarray, why his face has fallen so. If
there is a reason to clean out the sink, I

should be notified. Virgil Moon, with your
thick face, grab me by my ankles and
make a wish. Play my heart like a
terrible, hot fiddle, replace me with catgut,
and see what I'll look like come Monday
morning. Virgil Moon, you are over the top
and smell like canned beans. Virgil Moon
with the top down, making his travel plans
to the museum and the beach. Virgil Moon
takes back the ring. Spit me out sideways,
somewhere near a track where dogs are
supposed to race, and place your bets against
me. I will disappoint.

The Government Finance Officers Association

Today there has been a prediction of snow,
up to half a foot by midnight, and the air
is full of this possibility. If this were a poem,
by the end, the snow would begin to fall,
noiselessly, blanketing even the busiest
streets in this city with its cold wet.

There would be details about sad people
in tall office buildings, waiting for something
to change, how they floss after lunch with
thread and paperclips, how their teabags slap
the sides of their least favorite mugs, light one-
night stands trying to deserve something more,
how the whispered promise of pie or the cookies
on the seventh floor can move them from their

windows long enough to miss the sky becoming
whiter and the wind picking up litter from the
streets. After a lunch break too tedious to
surreptitiously extend, city of maudlin-slashed
villages, this could stick, I tell you.

Album

Here, in this one, you can see
coughing sequences, the next
room over.

There is writing you cannot read.
You will still try to, and the order
you arrive at, in, will stun you.
You were with him.
You had to stop crying.

You hissed and sometimes mewled
for what would not amount. You are
still waiting in this one, for the
other shoe, for boomerangs to undo
great distances.

Here you were turning away, towards
him. The cork-soled shoes were still
in style. And Mister Fever came—in this
one, with cheap scotch—not willing to
remove his gloves before crawling into
the bed.

Hibernation would have seemed a welcome
friend then. Forget what happened but
remember what names sounded like.
You have never wanted this, but are
tired of looking, and, what's more,
you are extraordinary at it.

Dinner—March

"...there is no such thing as adventure.
There's no such thing as romance.
There's only trouble and desire."
—from Hal Hartley's "Simple Men"

Another stoic dinner of cold spells;
make up your mind, or watch me climb

out this false window, a swatch
of your coat watches me leave this world,

slowly. Slipping out from a dress,
grime-streaks stay on my mind.

The best I can hope for is kindness,
for knowledge waves from a photograph.

You renew the problems of attempt,
the conditions of silence, of sound

amazement. It is a wonder, anyone
who survives. Our linen hostess takes

her seat. The cup pushes harder
against the saucer. In your mind

is the greatest picture of any subject
forgotten. One doubles over

with ailments undisclosed. Almost,
except. If it is true, so are we, free. Eviscerated,

turtle-headed snake, light shadows its own
movements, care of: fantasy acorn,

manipulation of geometry, and why not,
art of exploration. The pit of the world

is something you think
you have seen. After learning

to read, we rarely look around
when walking. We are visually

illiterate. Unraveled, unravished,
we will come loose in that air.

The Aged Gymnast Pauses Before the Vault

Who strains against the bars and the looseness of the grips.
The new point system eludes us all, nor was time fair.
The one thing I didn't want to be over is over when I am

over my own head. Focus instead on my lips, from whose
gashes emerge cyclones of locusts. I miss my 3-D leotards,
my beautiful white teeth performing the Yurchenko, every

turn a reminder of Friendship Games, so little given to
daughters and fathers outside the apparatus each skipped.
I felt like a goddess and aged like a homunculus. Whatever

happened to the living people? The hugs we exchanged were
handcuffs dropped around shoulders and ribcages dented.
We were penalized for venturing outside our boundaries.

Flipping on a four-inch beam, be a predator, my coach told
me. Carry your spine to your ears. Think of the papers waiting
for you afterwards to sign: begin with photos of yourself,

then balances and checks bigger than sleeping bags. I wanted
a fortress from my body. I disappeared in the smallest amounts.
I threw myself. I landed badly, but no one saw. I went nowhere.

A Dissimulation of Hummingbirds

"It's Nature, and it's Nothing. It's all Nothing."
E.A. Robinson

Size

Entryway, the man in the doorway
murmured, or maybe it was incubator,
what you'd call those willing to hold
sixty-two hummingbirds, none bigger
than the common marshmallow, unmelted,

apodiformes, never meant to walk or to rest.

Consider: resting hummingbirds riding
raindrops to gramophones, heralding
concepts like sullenly perfumed lovers
from beyond the pale. Sideways, they
revise their patterns and pray for light.

Flight

If you believe in goodness, you might soar
too quickly above derelict meadows; you
will not discuss your more palpable doubts.
If you land badly, no one else need know it.
Consider: people who want things can

make them happen. This could become

an instance of unhappy happenstance:
a new car breaks down outside a wearily
abandoned farmhouse; a bewilderment of
asides better known as riches; restless charms
in exchange for the renewed magic of belief.

Longevity

You will find ways to keep yourself lean
and alone. Those the hummingbirds love
know better than to die young. Those called
by hummingbirds never see themselves
measured but know this means the longer

you can live, relief will find you in its roots,

like a pando of feathers, a radiant pipeline,
salvation piped in, unrelenting. The humming-
bird's instrument is a dulcimer made from
the back shell of a screaming naked armadillo.
Birds in the basket are worth less than at home.

Nest & Eggs

Laid end to end, seven million hummingbird
eggs will take you to the bus stop and back.
Represent: Pierce's Disease, glassy wings,
the end of a new wine crop. You can't face
yourself anymore. You don't go out. You

don't allow for the provisions and machinations

provided by time itself. The incubation lasts
less time than the conception. Is it true? If
possible, the lightness should be kept along
the front, so as not to tip. You, my secret and
favorite, must always live in the background.

Feeding & Metabolism

Merely with their desperate wing patterns,
the hummingbirds try remembering their
other lives from their own photos: four
hummingbirds riding a baseball, a quaint
collection of flight feathers and ticket stubs.

You must wonder when they are allowed

moments to rest, to decrease the speed
of hyperphagia, a fragment of moon
will not give of itself, loosely veiled,
this sun reflecting its own pallid excuses,
rays delirious and poised above the lawn.

Migration & Site Fidelity

Hummingbirds on bicycles, humming-
birds on ice skates, hummingbirds
finding other ways of getting to speed.

Hummingbirds in dress whites, busy
piloting their chariots and armies of

earthworms against a foot threatening

to crush this landscape that continues
to breathe, despite its pan-suspicious naiveté.
Hummingbirds juggling pins afire, sporting
human teeth and lips, hummingbirds breast-
fed and full. You, let us fear them together.

How to Create Your Own Amnesia

Across your rutting chest, a carnage too
lovely for words. Like vacuums, your eyes
in the dark slink into autumn.

It was no secret I'd become
a person who fixes things.

Your face awesome in the snow.

Remember how I'd become what you'd make
me whisper into

you win. You grow a beard.
Your name is a swear word.

I am somewhere between the room and the city.

Notes Left Behind for the Zookeeper

One

I was serpentine in that light
away from you, spearing desire
with fourteen generations of forked
and predictable tongues. I have
aged a thousand graveyards,
carrying different possessions
with me each time. For luck,
a handful of sawdust, calling,
"ollie, ollie, oxen free" and going
home alone. Leave me this
shot-put and a field in which
to practice my self-exterminations
distraction free and sulking in
the corner. Leave my knuckles
alone. Without them, I cannot
measure my age, terminal moraine,
you know what you've not heard of.
The light I love you in lacks focus,
not intensity, the scene I'd seen seemed
sad. Do not ask me for anything
you'd want. Do not charm me
with your hint of rosemary, what that
meant once and what it means
now is cold. Come to me exhausted
and missing another tooth; I will fashion
you something in a burlap pellet. If
you believed me, I'd no longer be
believable. Come to me under the guise
of salve, the genius of a tweed jacket, the

fountain pen of a left-handed man, the impact
of need. You know better than to
offer protection, and perhaps I will die
thinking of your ears, the tongue
of Harry Houdini a dreamsicle, and we
have been fucking for four days. I tell you
a code is a way of saying my love
for you has disappeared, and there is nothing
here but the magic of a bleached bone, a shard
of something larger. The dresser is too much
for the naked eye. There could be a coat
on that rack. You'd think anything possible.

Two

The smell of you is so good you should
get a medal. It is harder to love a baseball
player with his allegiances changing like
colors and letters and you have no higher
average than the last at-bat, that is to say,
you are not a baseball player. How badly
they want. How I would like to be
lost in whatever comes before dark, a guitar
riff, a shovel-nosed landlady who loved
your scent, too, and would bring you
overcooked milk every morning on her
way to no place, who raised you to wait
until she was gone before pouring it out,
watching the liquid struggle to break
through the top skin layer? Oh, but

these are slow days, and I watch
for things I never expected to see:
kudzu, these flacons on the shelf,
gasoline-fierce, the commodity
of loss, Dolomite chips in my soufflé,
there is a reason for this lightness
and soon I will forget it, though these daisy
petals, shredded, when you throw them,
they fall down like white liquid would.

Three

Every noise must happen for a reason.
Things hit one another. In one hour,
I will be alone, proving I have been weak
around my endings. There is nothing to buy
for this. Not maybe, she's signing, yes.
Swing wildly around, plunger-like
arms, the wildest teeth floating in the canoe's
moraine, and she has left, no signs of
crystal balls, the myth of sunflowers
following that god, the one who didn't
listen until he was done crossing, got
home, and sank into those cushions.
Still, there is much to read, and while
I will not watch a sunset without
thinking of how a sunset looks, I would
cross the street and can vegetables
with my smile. What went into her
was not worth it. A phone that rings
at such an hour should not be picked up.
Who knows, noise, empty bodies clattering

against each other in some horrible
other light, one in absentia, but this is how
to place her, this is where to put
your hand, I say, and the summer of you
is slow, halcyon, daddy, what you need
limps, bravely, curbward-bound.

Four

My skin is that of a chicken, and I am rotting
from both inside and out. When she stood
in front of that tiny house, it looked bigger.
You could call this perspective. Put me
in a scene and watch as nothing changes.
I am looking down on something and it is
my life and I cannot love it. No powders or
herbs for this wretched little heart, so evil
your tongue might stick if you touched
it to it. I will not bounce, wind myself
through my own capillaries, waiting for each
tiny vein pulsing like schoolyard double dutch
before entering, the rhythms are the same, the
same, and both spell out something which looks
like me. Oh, but I am going down so
badly. Look, lean in to warm yourself and
draw away, hair singed around the important part.

Dear Baby, Love Here Is Cornfed

I am breezing through this town on the strength
of my tone and my unstoppable urge for shoplifting.
Such are the limitations of the untrained zealot: he
is in hiding, and what about the body?
You huge stupid cold dead body with
the voice that sounded like the wind against
a cheekbone, I'll lift my glass in memory
of thee in a motel by that lake and a shallow pool,
bulky with your wine and too much brightness. Weighed
down, I have heard that your elders smoked cornsilk
wrapped in cornhusks. I have heard the taste
of condensation. The quality of my skin is lessening,
an endangered species, and you go for it: that ashtray,
the one outside filled with twigs, changeling birds
and smoke. I was never last. I will only embrace
what does not embrace me, and this is the truth,
even if you hate me. Dear Baby, I am held up
by anchors and antlers: one holds me down, the other
keeps me alone. I am dead blue, love. Sometimes,
in other countries, people sleep less because things start
later, their dreams obscured by what they must do
in daylight hours. To those who wish to be cold and should
not move too often, away from sandalwood, keep but
one hand under your coats, holding in your sad little
hearts, to where do you stray? So long and melancholy,
not every connection will make sense and you must
accept this, Baby, with your electric typewriter,
your mountains of peeled grapes, islands brought
downstream to you, three things you need like another
bloodied year. Left out, right doesn't matter.
You say you see you don't. That version of love

takes up too much space in this kind of a bedroom.
You could stretch yourself from wall to ceiling,
floor meets closet, and you are already planning
the next place. At the end of this night, a slow-
moving bug will alight on your forearm and you
decide not to go for that walk and instead pull
plastic-smelling sheets you know nothing about
tighter around and know you have a dirty bad heart
and will never know the things people tell you, do, you do.

I Love How Your Eyes Close Every Time You Kiss Me

a variation on a line from a song by Bobby Vinton

You are alone and you are easy. You see
the history of your life and lineage in your
mitochondrial genes, confirming what
we suspected: bottleneck, enlargement, plague,
vulcanologists from everywhere, studying the
site, thinking aren't you a cute disease. The
music is so loud you blink every time there is
a drum. Yes, best we heirloom quietly, for we
are powerful weak. Overcoat, spread your wings.
Almost a legend, knots laced with passed-over
glass, daddies in pastel suits next to the only
surviving witness from a life best spent in big
dreams of sliding on your belly. Tough night,
wet ink, loose seams. Time allotted is never
enough. Roll over and tell me you're a sofa,
backboned by an old quilt, tied to the notion
of design, of pattern, of words so staccato they bang
like rats atop the roofs of government embassies,
that is, without regard for what those below will
try to assume you are: harmless and preoccupied,
known through your gestures to be true.
The ropey cuisine of another planet awaits you
tonight, something freeze-dried and wet
just for you, and molded into whatever you
want: lids and caps, some beans or rice, coelacanth,
but the remains will leave their fossils
on your plate. Memory is like this, patterns

already laid out across neurons and blisters,
each occasion that follows will fit
into that shape, even sans arms or eyelashes,
rendered sharp-tongued with bad desire.

[when I say *backdoor* I mean the way a lot]

When I say backdoor, I mean the way a lot
of young hitters begin, afraid and ready to bolt,
a wooden bat beaten up. The room,
the sun, the sky, the moon put up last. The barn,
the beach, the metalworks, the shed. When we say lazy eye,
it means if only it had ever wanted to see.

Consider the eardrum, rolled like a fiddlehead fern,
inserted into another's ear like a tractor with a metallic
tip, extended into another discipline, a phantom brain,
Laura dolls with their eyes popped out. Fifteen incalculable
years calculated: a new diving facility.
Forty-four facial muscles in humans; the dead
serve the living; they know we're nothing special.

Your giant food's no good here, honey.
Your liver is connected only to you. Your head stares directly.
You know of reeds that have waited, collecting themselves for years.
And there's the husband, anyone's guess.
You say, runners go but do not mean it much.
It is a better way to get what we need, to find space.

When I say backdoor, I mean the world, I mean
come freely and of someone else's volition. I mean
it meanly and with no teeth. I mean it until I no longer
can mean it.

Summer Crookneck

The lake was beautiful and low, its surface pulled
so tight in places like chenille, it condensed, it stained,
remnants of roman candles and bottle rockets, phylogenetic
victims of an undefined and patriotic malaise.
My words are undoing me doing this work.
Through the rememorized surface,
nothing is pushing against nothing.

A drought should end as slowly as it started.
There's no molding to this leg room, no shaking
free of superstition, rags with shirts around their edges.
Looking away is not enough. Start on the second floor;
withhold your eyes from entering. Built like a sand
castle, suckers for calamity, like we are going along with
this dead idea. Wickedness pushes me onwards. What we say:

nothing, and thusly, it vanishes. The distance between things,
between inappropriately understated eyes is far, hardly worth
trying to touch tongue to it. I ask for stratification and I mean
the clouds. There are many holes to a face. Pay special
attention to how the eyes continue following the trajectory
of the dropped object, even following its recovery.

Tell me how to get you back, awareness and shame.
Speak to me speech so regular I can tell when
you'll miss the words. Autotroph, you are eating
my bones apart. Every day I see you for the first
time. How do we allow ourselves this openness?
It will not be you who catches my backwards motion
of yes. There is nothing between us but space.

Kansas City Still Life

It was likely to have been three days after the murder
that a man with a hose stood in the driveway washing
the phantoms of both the car and the corpse that rested
behind its wheel. It was likely to have been the dura

mater that protected the brain but killed the body. It
was a second, it was a stranger's hand in the garage;
it was the son who appeared standing near the driveway.
It was the sound of firecrackers that were not firecrackers.

It was the sound of a woman screaming that can sound
like a child. A child can sound like a cat. Hierarchically
is how things will themselves to sleep. It was thirty days
of showers to rid the concrete of the organics, the horrors

of suburbia, the lawns stretched like models who have learned
their joy from seedy catalogues. By the second day, it is
likely that the blood no longer flows from a wound, but still
holds its body up. It was likely you were asleep. Tell me

what your memory allows you to see: a sign on your back:
never stop kicking. Enjoy yourself, the tyranny of intentions,
enter now, dear Cousin Apathy, the return for the second cup,
the hand on the shoulder, the invitation, the demurral. When

we met, there was a graveyard involved, a good place for wincing.
Tell me whodunit and move on. It is the decision of the body.
My friends hiding in the ceiling. No one was surprised when it
happened again. Look, the court orders. His face was on fire.

Notes Left Behind for the Bellboy

Bellboy, be warned of my terrible love
for your few useful services. A new mythology
forecasts: one stray glove means you will walk
on foreign soil. A drunken heiress means
you've been around too long and will go
nowhere. A man with sweat stains soaking
through before noon brings no good;
your dreams tonight involve cutlery, papier mâché.

I will play the remnants, pieced together,
of a grande dame. You should treat me
as such. This is not how I will go. Not
quietly. Push away whatever you would
have expected to come. Your scars are such
women, pressing themselves against. I could love
you and your kind, efficient fleets in hallways predictable
and stairwells, pausing to brush away mildewed towels
underfoot, something nipping at your ankles.

The last baggage you bring up bulges with glue
batons and moonrats, their voices metallic, jaded,
even at their surprising and fictitious demise. The air
in my mouth is fog-bitter. My handwriting
would break your heart. I want more:
empty bodies clattering light and quiet,
and I will tell you where to put that hand
luggage. I dare you. Like signs
too blatant to ignore in a B movie, sensory
overload, if you play your cards right, Bellboy,
we'll be living under timed hot lights,
my head under water for hours.

There is a code you need not follow,
guiding without authority, but with
the heartbreaking precision of a broken record
player stuck on the highest notes. This is what
will make you choose, will claw at you
demanding limestone resolution
and the best ways to lose three teeth
at midnight in a bad part of town with people you'd do better
not to recognize in the lobby. There is a change
in the music and it is called a bridge.

The Sex Lives of Clowns

Oh the unexpected way
in which we grow accustomed
to the loss of metallic weight,
steeled by love, something flutters
not in my chest, but here, here
is where my sickness falls from
its trees, my glaucous inflorescence
leaves its leaves, traces everywhere.

If not for this rain of diamonds,
we could be on Neptune, dodging
air that weighs upwards and promises
new roads and doesn't deliver. Oftentimes,
the hands of children smell of wooden
benches you could lick safely and
make rude gestures in the mornings
there; you could flannel words through
counterfeit bricks. They are colder than
weather. The night is conducive.

Rarely are the unfortunate so lovely
as their penance. It is too late. Like you,
they're infamous and cold blooded, eyes
like neon, flashing open, flashing open,
daring you to look away. You love them.
They never change. Puffy under the skin,
necks surprisingly slender, infinitesimally small
ways of picking up on change. They become
preoccupied with speed, with leaves in sick.

In Venice, the boats would take you
home. In Chicago, I take you.
You will find them, better than
mimes, furiously pacing, chewing
on wires fit only for small landfills. Oh,
how they suspend desire, childlike poses,
words so fancy, and something gaping
at you in the darkness afterwards. There is little
to laugh at, and less in the way of beauty.

Things like this and clowns are everywhere.
I am trapped in Chicago, veering from Noble
to Division, or meaning to veer. Because
I do not know, there are things like clowns,
the sky hollowing itself from the sweatiest crevasse.
Everything burns that leaves.
The skyline repeats, I am taken lightly. I am
taken lightly. Remember me as
this punch line: a man walks in and says nothing.

The Vanishing Room

Says that it's why we always carry
our people on one side. Cantilevered,
pulled back like that, what costs us
one point, one heart means we handle
like libras, deducted from and acclimated

to the appearance of this camera. Say
it's something in the sky and we will miss
it. Say it's something in a painting that floats
its way past a series of arms moving too
quickly for it. If you wait, we might then

say it's yes, but watch me; I'll run out of ice.
The hardest jumps are always the ones after
falls, ice adjacent to, say, the marrow on
its subsequent tailspin, that graceless lady
changed her music from stripped to a distant

mention, to not crying enough, to the fresher
of the offered towelettes. Say, we are beauty
away from school. Across not one but four deserts,
the wires connect us in slow gestures, which
is better than saying not at all and this might be

over soon and sometimes in dreams, you might,
say, the reverse of a hawk is a zephyr, that what
design is good for includes the remedial additions
of bombs into tables, frozen into kitchens too near
those very heat sources they eschewed. Say, what I

want moves west of me. Who is to say I would
even want it back, or that I might want to sleep
against the back of your back, that is, back
before your milk teeth and shoes, those saints
merged in terrible photographs, shadows of, say,

puppets, fit to be stoned to death in rooms
of their own makings. Say, thank you, for
company, in this empty non-mobile non-home,
for the names of the four true alien genders
(right, left, squid, helper), for the imagined

forcings over the imaginary table, the call, say,
that never extends itself to the performance,
what porcelain cannot do, the muscles that,
when knotted, look back like cats across a series
of stubborn and obstacular interventions.
What we wanted was less than, say, less
than that. Realize. Your guards are downed
by the work that goes into each breath. Say,
the background seems back to where we
met, began, back during the times our bodies

wore different clothes and met at the, say, the same
places. We miss our flight not because we
are not there, but due to the overdue hands of
this new shame. There is disappointment here. I
always wanted you to see me this way, fading

towards light, your punishment, giant, floating
or otherwise, say, to suffer me.

An Accident Waiting to Happen

To you, the hard porn king about to start
a series of shots beneath the ankle,
the foot more important than your cock:
wait for it. Someone will come.

Horrible guitar chords, Esteban
with his exciting news, eponymous
the plumber, extreme the yank
and thrust of his wrenches into

the sinkhole. Beloved are his tangents.
Beloved are the ways teeth are known
to take care of themselves. We
have them like friends we ignore long

enough to make them go. The body,
prone, steamy, the mise-en-scène.
The first step is meeting the surgeon.
The last thing anyone does is clean

the floor. You ask about keeping
strong. You slip the keyhole matte
onto the front of the camera. The
extraordinary stretch makes it solid.

It makes the feet hidden. Don't call
it anything prettier than what it is.
Your hands are what hold the fists out.
Your mouth wants its words back in.

Dialogue for Robots

We are alone and we are afraid to be.
We do not need to be told what is missing from our lives, or where it went.

Our hairplates gleam like roaches in this just-born light.
In front of our eyes are too many ways to breathe.

We wish to be admired for our glossolalia and our knowledge of foreign
    architecture.
We are aware of erotica and its place next to the hearth.

One thing we want still is a dainty pitcher shaped like one of our babies.
The last thing we touched abandoned its shape betwixt our mighty fingers.

We are relieved and we are nonchalant.
We know it is illegal in Maine to own an armadillo.

One problem might be that when you can fly, it means you can't swim.
If you could suck the marrow from your own bones, it might ask you not to stop.

We wish to remain together afterwards.
We wish our dreams to stay with us longer.

Fifteen Beautiful Colors

I. Four mornings in a row of dawns, reversed sunsets, greasepaint reflections of peril heightened.

II. Ash, scattered, tastes of care and warns of inter-mural collisions. Expected, their flat hues.

III. Speaker, formulaic, blends all domestics into hard-won remainders like salt and rock salt.

IV. Lights at their brightest are the first to be extinguished. Six tickets rigged. Stained clandestine yellow.

V. Signals, misfired. Cornflower becomes alabaster, what voices scrape the self-professed neutron into action.

VI. Sweets, water, rested and longing for motion, the completion of the voiced projections: picture, abandon.

VII. My love, this journey and you have worn me like a jacket, like bluish seams erased and easily worn out.

VIII. Comfortable lead, pulling from center together, narrow as spit rope. Forty bowls, none glass.

IX. No one cares for the plights of the professionals, their amber sweat, their safety is what this does for you.

X. This is what the conversation looks like when no one wants to have it. Someone keeps score in red.

XI. Dead pull hitter. No trigger. Even the handle has been sold. What remains, iron.

XII. Two arms reaching make little sound grasps at smoke. Nothing here will bloom or rise, planetary faces.

XIII. Ball into glove is to tincture as impact was to need. Precious intensity wheedles its own sins.

XIV. Fine and ground to pieces no bigger than the heart of palm that holds yours. Waves out, be mine.

XV. What is this moon but silver ending, this flesh but nothing, this lamp, this stiff night.

Figure Skating

Frozen marvels, you never should have counted on me.
Each time, we are the dinosaurs' bones disassembled.
This is not what I had in mind. A member for the week,

I waited for your call. With its black lingering
window-dwelling sheets, your bed was not meant
to be slept in. I watched hours of spiral sequences,

axels and salchows, and I'll say I judged in secret.
My results were never tallied. To wear your bones on
the outside lets the silver whisper what we once almost

were, the bronze simply lies. Watch me straighten
your tie, switch from axel to toepick and it's too bad
to see any rotation implode on its surface, a play

we play at by lifting to some higher note no one
forgets to wait for. O stars, the kiss and cry, artful,
the awful dodging of hands, the night that hangs

with desire over ice, the evening's what we wait for,
along with the beauty of the lines. You cannot but make
the perils of living alone seem worse than those of seeing

imaginary people built with real eyes, raised to be
themselves by invisible gestures. It is like coming,
only backwards, the blind landing has its own leaps.

Appetite

After Denis Johnson's "Surreptitious Kissing"

No room for tenderness
in a bathroom, only bodies

so tenuous that to touch them
is an economy of words and

an appetite that buckles
like please say nothing

if you must and asks the hand
to touch the face, against me,

tell me, things I want badly:
outside, this evening, inside

a phantom series, discarded
planetary faces like transparent

mirrored gluttons, and I introduce
myself as I should have been:

breezy and simple, lost in spaces
no bigger than the heart's feigned

gesture, now so lewd, that this
would be something you might

on some other time or this place
remember me worth forgetting.

The Problem with Night Stories

To remember teenagers sneaking into moneyed places
is to believe the night capable of blooming around you,
obscene with its extra pistils, magicians saying If you act

like something you become it. Like you, only clockwise,
the fable disappears into the water without ripple,
as though some clocks might still, would lower

their faces against the wind and pass me. As though
you lived here, I will iron everything harder, as though
I knew how iron can be fashioned, soldered to locks

unopened, cautioned against fire, against wet snow,
bringing you to the older brother's armchair, spider legs
splayed for the benefit of this darkening hearth. I trust

we will both be on our worst behavior, our well-being
invisible in the loyal daytime, a rehearsal for the evening's
ticker-tape of betrayals. She is the middle girl, an odd man

out of time, happy for me, crossing the international
date line. They say Madrid is the highest capital
in Europe, when for me it meant your car's backseat.

Let me go out of me, genius of limbless locomotion,
if you've not got enough proof, then it cannot be proven.
What is important is that everyone gets out alive.

From the Monster Nights

It is so nice to think of you, rappelling with bed sheets,
or without, tied around your middle and tied to one end
of a bed framed with photos of barbells from the days
of great holy mastiffs, along with wallets, soup cans, ribbons

from fashion girls in the eighties, sported, braided three times
around one common frame. What is right for you, out the
window with flowers and the last of your attempts to harvest
love and the people and the speed and the noise, and I'm more

than scared of you. If there is time, I want you to limit the dogs
in the alley, the focal points of motion, a refusal which will no
longer speak your name. Tell me the best exits, the worst dirty way

of putting lip to neck, angelic stupid fingers stubby and pugnacious
as an old lamb's knees; yes to the promise of the sex, wet and mild
as grass in the morning, tea at night, and melted rubber in between.
Still, I love you better for your absences. It is bad days I see ahead.

Anymore, I surrender to your terrible love, never alone except
with you. In dreams, you turn towards me and no more accidents
happen. In dreams, the splinters of you tweeze themselves out;
the mailbox empties itself of bad news; the birds sing again,

only slightly less themselves. I cannot believe this is where I find
myself, lace shawls lately, gloves waiting only like me for being put on.
We breathe out, neither gain nor loss nearby.

Junkyard Dinner

Nothing worth imagining can be seen
there, hideous in rust, neglectful and

fortunate, allowed to drive in, sold and given
up, handed down, laid like the parts of doll

porcelain attached by threads of gentle blood,
bodily ropes capable of hoisting deposits,

come back again tonight, touch yourself
under the steering column, pretend these

needs are political to your nature. Tell
anyone you know. Changes are candles

held upside down. They burn, and in
their refusals, you can see their doing:

coming to bed, burning out alighted
upon, put out, understanding, wired

with me. You can take the stairs or else
shiver under this metal canopy. Let me

finger your ratted cushions once more, graze
under the hood, a taste, the notion of tongue,

bitten through, and though it seems an act
of silence, I'd say this is a man speaking

now to me and for all purposes dead.
If, as they say, flipping over a shark

hypnotizes it, what then happens to cars
driven into upside down traffic patterns,

into the artifice of this done-him-wrong-

shut-mouth. This is a poem with no dogs
in it. This is words held heavenly to your head.

The Halo Effect

The algebra of our bodies is always
here. With us, it is the exhalation
of space, the bites we take from
many things. In this picture, everyone
looking to the right will be saved.

Nothing was important but us,
the concern, the languages,
all percentages of the loss. I have
been studying your silent organisms,
these islands filled with relative families.

If you can imagine so many people
saying the same things in different
languages, you can understand the
economy of an airport and how
the people in it will be arranged.

Impatient people have no business
planting trees. Next: a spider plant's
roots, evil white glistening and cracking
open their containers. Tell it, say be
good when no one is meant to be watching.

Elegy In The Absence Of

By the second day, cheating becomes
the maiden, easier than playing honestly
burnt bones against dishonest bones who
think everything means the world, fiercely
grasping at the most hapless of weeds.

If, by the twenty-nine-hundredth day,
love continues following rules, surrender
becomes impossible. Nine years of news,
of the same thoughts, the reports, bug-
eyed and tender, evil and hot, a see with

no saw, a language for robots, a series of
ragged readings. Something is coming
to an end. The gift of assignments has
no need for a future, for a threat, or for
redemption. The over-textured air around

the people stays white. There is nothing
left to say. Names will not be remembered.
Lives have made no difference. Everything
is game for reconsideration: the heads
of Renaissance painters jousting tumors

from lips to bones, unlucky unlucky
unlucky unlucky, since 1530, since January,
since the end, since love has never been
enough, since everything is a question.
Try catching a tumbling birdcage, bouncing

from bottom to top, following the path
of a runaway resident, a coop flung by
the bird, the nuisance of belonging to a camp
that advocates the enclosures of love: closets,
blinded and folded, terror at dawn, and maybe.

Life is worth a mouthful of blood.
Pretend things are happening now.

Elegy Next to Cleanliness

This backyard has been a haven for vipers.
There is so much about snakes I did not
know. They, if permitted, are liable to dry-
bite rather than waste venom on a warm rat

staggering, already poisoned across rows
of chairs useless to it. The viper's hollow
fangs are what inspired the hypodermic needle.
Venom is pumped in, welcome it, this cocktail,

its dozens of ingredients convening to liquefy
your tissue and when silence comes, you
might remember it as what you'd asked for, to milk
these, your captive vipers, to be handled like

nothing less than pearl-handled toothbrushes.
One week after missing my grandmother's
funeral, I'll attend one for a girl I never met.
I'll became one, viper of the pocketbook, two,

thieves of photos, three ruined families around
an oak table, all remembered as the last reckonings
of an unfairness gone beyond what is possible, what
is speakable, what means regret more than a father

who fucks then kills his daughter. It is wrong to have
wanted you then. There, your face as imagined clean
by my viper lips in its and their openings more naked than
in coming, more needful than the hard casket indoors.

The warmth I'll feel will not be mentioned. Your suit
will smell correctly and vexingly of rot. You will cry
behind panoramic eyes. You will put your fingers
in my mouth to prove you were not afraid of loss.

The heroine in each child's story will be kissed
somewhere special: behind the ears, under
the tongue, across the scars left behind by
a vitriolic landscape. We will let ourselves see these

caresses, raise them, and believe ourselves normal.
We will later shroud ourselves within a sequence
of richnesses, of pallors so defining they explain
their own contributions to a funeral. I am trying

to protect you, says the inscription on the ring.
I stole it from a dish in the bathroom and denied
it later, the grieving and forgetful aunt left
rubbing her empty finger with its ring divot

cutting first through her finger, then into the bone.

The Superstition of the Clean Glass

A cross-section of a tough person seems
touched in the middle of an island, and
we like it. No matter how hard we tried,

your cheek is required in exchange.
Any tongue will be sacrificed for the sake
of the sour. Two hands will be filled with

garbage, filed without caution in a cabinet
without curiosity or folders, the companions
of your childhood: your trombone, your

Suzuki Method, your guitars' protection
against bad news, things you wish would
turn true. You are most beautiful from any

distance that allows the audience to avert its
eyes. How brave and dangerous to use a glass
at all, to cleanse the rim, dreamy with lip-mute

bridles, to raise the heretic's fork lipwards,
to lie down on the unmade bed in the made-
up house, to burn your fingers on the turban-

shaped nightlight. The last glass swallowed
you whole, each memory taken out like
a burned-out bulb: with care only for what

happens when dropped, yet utterly useless: sixty-
five gallons of orange glaze in a blue pick-up truck,
the fifth leg of a lonesome cat, the horse imposters,

the other sides of fruit, the last time we were chased,
a farm outside Ohio, confirming in your mind the
things you thought you wanted to think. Some of you

went shopping. Your feet avoided cracks. In the sick
bad darkness, you were the bad sick darkness, the ragged-
tooth shark turning three times in the entryway every

time it swallows. Cobwebs, massive and empty,
you've had your chance. Your heart is perfect.
If you can picture it, I'll meet you there.

The Oversized World

There is always time to choose new curtains. What to
keep: a light-bulb the size of the city, a tank bent on

reconstruction, pilots and bubbles, sixty-one ways
to evacuate a twin with a twin with more twins in it.

Imaginary babies ask for organic juice and whole milk.
I wait for each day to be over. I am the breaker of

interrogations. Remember: everything is a test. See
who protects you now, gardener of leaves, leaver of

sleeves, creator of estate jewelry and actual sizes. If you
remember, everything looks like it should be in motion.

Out-of-step, following inconstant signals and misfired
fires onto pages made of ham. The oversized world

passes its scream-test. The oversized world pulls out
its knife, but only for show. It's like your bones died two

weeks before you did. People are saved when no one
notices they are there. Think how things shrink from

cold. Not just things, but *things*. We are retreating
from the touch of a hand equally unsure, hypnosis, its

static, its stasis, its desire to be drawn, to be filled-in.
Something will be built, bulleted, discussed, danced

a light two-step through, the naked, the pale, the
please stay here, the one who prefers to be with me.

It's like taking down glass from a window. The
blessings have been blocked. The men stand around,

talking lawsuits out of their necks' creases,
saying, Here, baby, let me do something for you.

The Humiliation Parade

on evolution and photography

How brave and dangerous you are
to select this audience, then to suggest
it close its eyes. How beautiful you are

from such a great distance, brandishing
the heretic's fork, alarming scales
scaling disappointing heights of desire.

Yes, but the water is in you, inflections
of an organist, happy-go-lucky and discreet.
We love people who cannot keep secrets.

We have secrets we make our own, the
language, the percentage, the concern,
the fortress. I have been studying your

secret organisms, piloting your armies,
collecting locusts and oven birds. Each
pain-filled island is filled with its own

closest relatives, with barnacles living
and fossils, tumbler pigeons one step
closer to something that began with E

and ended with you, spinning, directly,
the bottle only pointing at you, warbling
ant bird, monosyllabic and comforting

to some. I have studied the morphology
of your bills, the sample corpses lined up
in immobile panic. Not everything has

been said. We still have creatures who
can swallow us whole. We are ragged
beneath. Stop. I'll show you a picture.

[We have to be mean, my uncle]

We have to be mean, my uncle
says to the garbage bag of things

my grandmother kept. We look
through them with the television

on. An outfielder who looks over
his head loses sight of the ball.

The score does not matter. What
the bag held does not matter, but

it was jewelry and it was pictures
and they wanted it thrown away.

It is the responsibility of the utterance
which prevents us from making it.

It is a melting tree that feels no rain.
It is love the true carrier of sound.

ACKNOWLEDGMENTS

"Notes Left Behind for the Bellboy" and "Notes Left Behind for the Zookeeper" appeared in *Keep Going*, Winter 2003, No. 10.

"Moonrats" and "Bunny Ohio" appeared in *The Canary*, 2003, Volume 2.

"The Sex Lives of Clowns" appeared in *Keep Going*, Spring 2003, No. 11.

"Like a Face" appeared in *Can We Have Our Ball Back?*, 2003, No. 17.

"Anne Boleyn" appeared in *Gulf Coast*, Winter/Spring 2004, Vol. 16, No. 1.

"Pavese Said Death Will Come Bearing Your Eyes" appeared in *26*, 2004, April.

"Virgil Moon" appeared in *Black Warrior Review*, Spring/Summer 2004, vol. 30, No. 2.

"I Love How Your Eyes Close When You Kiss Me," appeared in *Bridge*, August/September 2004.

"Summer Crookneck" and "How to Create Your Own Amnesia" appeared in *Backwards City Review*, 2004, Volume One, No. One.

"Dear Baby, Love Here Is Cornfed" appeared in *Gulf Coast*, Winter/Spring 2005, Vol. 17, No. 1.

"Loud" appeared in *Court Green*, 2005, Vol. 2.

"Darwin Light" appeared in *VOLT*, 2005, No. 11.

"63rd and Pulaski" appeared in *The Adirondack Review*, Spring 2005, Vol. 5, No. 2.

"Album" appeared in *Le Mot Juste*, 2005, June, No. 2.

"The Problem with Night Stories" and "Junkyard Dinner" appeared in *H_NGM_N*, 2006, Vol. 5.

"Nightdoctors" and "The Government Finance Officers Association" appeared in *The Iowa Review*, December 2006, Vol. 36, No. 3.

"Car Rolls Off Clay Wade Bailey Bridge" appeared in *The Boston Review*, 2007, January/February Vol 32, No. 1.

"A Dissimulation of Hummingbirds" and "Kansas City Still Life" appeared in *Canarium*, 2008, Vol. One.

"[we have to be mean, my uncle]" appeared in *Barn Owl Review*, Issue Two, 2009

"Elegy Next to Cleanliness" appeared in *Boxcar Review*, September 2009

"The Humiliation Parade" appeared in *13 Miles from Cleveland*, Volume 3, Number 1, 2010

"The Halo Effect" appeared in *Weave*, Issue 4, Spring/Summer 2010

"The Oversized World," "[when I say *backdoor* I mean the way a lot]" and "Elegy in the Absence Of" appeared in *The Iowa Review*, Spring 2011, Volume 41, Number 1.

Selected poems from this collection also appeared in *Between the Room and the City*, a chapbook from H_NGM_N B__KS, 2006.

Many, many thanks for your inspiration, guidance, friendship, and generosity: John Beer, Anna Marie Craighead-Kintis, Drew Dalton, Josh Edwards, Paul Guest, Lynn Hart, Rich Housh, David Kirby, Tammy Konieczko, Lisa Lapointe, Nate Pritts, James Reiss, Laura Romanoff, Alison Matthews Sampson, David Trinidad, Sarah Townsend, and Keith Tuma.

Thank you, David Dodd Lee.

Thank you to Keith, Marshi, Andrew, and Sophia Huneycutt, and to my wonderful colleagues and students at Florida Southern College.

To Suzanne Buffam, Michael Dumanis, Brian Harty, Mark Levine, Cate Marvin, Srikanth Reddy, Robyn Schiff, and Nick Twemlow: without you this book would not exist, and it is also dedicated to you, with love.

"The Vanishing Room" is for Brian Harty.

"Elegy in the Absence of" is for Diane Fagin Adler.

Photo by Drew Dalton

Erica Bernheim was born in New Jersey and grew up in Ohio and Italy.
She received her MFA from the University of Iowa's Writers' Workshop
and her PhD from the University of Illinois at Chicago. Since 2008, she
has been an Assistant Professor of English at Florida Southern College,
where she teaches creative writing and directs the Honors Program.